Clicks to Cash

The Complete Guide to Monetizing Your Social Media Presence"

M.A. Gorre

Contents

Introduction

Overview of Social Media Monetization

Social media monetization refers to the process of generating revenue through various activities and strategies on social media platforms. This has become a significant aspect of the digital economy, with platforms like Facebook, Instagram, TikTok, and Twitter offering numerous opportunities for individuals and businesses to earn money.

The Rise of Social Media as a Business Tool

The evolution of social media from simple communication platforms to complex ecosystems supporting business and commerce is a testament to their growing importance in our digital lives. Platforms have developed sophisticated algorithms and tools that enable users to reach large, targeted audiences, making them ideal for monetization.

Monetization Opportunities Across Platforms

Each social media platform offers unique features and audiences, leading to distinct monetization opportunities:

1. **Facebook**: Known for its vast user base, Facebook provides opportunities for monetization through Facebook Marketplace, sponsored content, and ads. It also supports businesses through Facebook Pages and Groups, which can be leveraged for brand building and sales.

2. **Instagram**: As a visually oriented platform, Instagram is ideal for influencers, brands, and creators who rely on imagery and videos. Monetization methods include sponsored posts, affiliate marketing, Instagram Shopping, and IGTV ads.

3. **TikTok**: TikTok's algorithm favors viral content, making it a powerful platform for influencers and creators. Monetization can be achieved through brand partnerships, sponsored content, and TikTok's Creator Fund.

4. **Twitter**: Twitter's strength lies in real-time engagement and information dissemination. Monetization comes through sponsored tweets, brand ambassadorships, and using the platform to drive traffic to monetized web content.

The Importance of a Targeted Approach

A successful monetization strategy on social media requires understanding the unique aspects of each platform and tailoring content accordingly. It's not just about posting content; it's about posting the right content for the right audience on the right platform.

Leveraging User Base and Engagement

The key to monetization lies in building and engaging with a loyal follower base. This involves consistently delivering valuable, relevant, and engaging content, and interacting with the audience to build trust and rapport.

Monetization Through Diverse Strategies

Monetization strategies in social media are diverse, ranging from direct sales and advertising to indirect methods like brand partnerships and affiliate marketing. Each strategy has its own set of best practices and success factors.

Challenges in Social Media Monetization

While the opportunities are vast, there are challenges too. These include platform algorithm changes, privacy concerns, market saturation, and the need for continuous content innovation.

The Role of Analytics in Monetization

Understanding social media analytics is crucial for effective monetization. Analytics provide insights into audience behavior, content performance, and ROI, enabling creators and businesses to refine their strategies for better results.

Ethical and Legal Considerations

Ethical and legal considerations are paramount in social media monetization. This includes adhering to platform policies, respecting copyright and intellectual property rights, and ensuring transparency with sponsored content.

The Future of Social Media Monetization

The future of social media monetization looks promising, with emerging trends like augmented reality (AR), virtual reality (VR), and the integration of e-commerce capabilities. Staying updated with these trends and adapting strategies accordingly is essential for continued success.

Conclusion

In conclusion, social media monetization presents a lucrative opportunity for those willing to invest time and effort into understanding and leveraging the unique aspects of each platform. With the right strategies, anyone from individual creators to large businesses can tap into the potential of social media to generate significant revenue.

Importance of Social Media in Today's Economy

Social media has revolutionized the way we communicate, interact, and conduct business, becoming a critical component in today's economy. Its influence extends across various sectors, impacting how companies market products, how consumers make purchasing decisions, and how information is disseminated globally.

1. Driving Consumer Behavior

Social media platforms wield significant influence over consumer behavior. They serve as hubs for reviews, recommendations, and user-generated content, all of which can sway purchasing decisions. Businesses leverage this by engaging in social media marketing to enhance brand visibility and reputation.

2. Marketing and Advertising Transformation

Traditional marketing and advertising methods have been transformed by social media. These platforms offer targeted advertising capabilities based on user data, allowing businesses to reach specific demographics more effectively and efficiently than ever before.

3. Economic Empowerment and Entrepreneurship

Social media has democratized the process of business creation and growth. Entrepreneurs and small businesses can now access global markets with minimal investment, leveling the playing field against larger corporations. The ease of reaching a wide audience has led to the emergence of countless online businesses and startups.

4. Influencer Economy

The rise of influencers is a direct result of the power of social media. Influencers, often individuals who have amassed large followings, can monetize their reach through brand partnerships, sponsored content, and product endorsements. This has created a new sector within the economy, where influence and audience engagement are commoditized.

5. Customer Engagement and Service

Social media has transformed customer service. Brands now use these platforms as tools for customer engagement, feedback, and support.

The direct interaction between businesses and consumers on social media enhances customer satisfaction and loyalty.

6. Data-Driven Insights for Businesses

Social media generates vast amounts of data, providing businesses with valuable insights into consumer preferences, trends, and behavior. This data is crucial for market research, product development, and strategic planning, making businesses more adaptive and responsive to market needs.

7. Job Creation and New Career Paths

The growth of social media has led to the creation of new job roles and career paths. Social media managers, content creators, digital marketers, and data analysts are just a few examples of positions that have emerged from the social media revolution.

8. Global Connectivity and Trade

Social media has broken down geographic barriers, enabling global connectivity. This interconnectedness facilitates international trade, cultural exchange, and collaboration across borders, contributing to a more integrated global economy.

9. Impact on News and Information Dissemination

The way people consume news and information has been fundamentally altered by social media. It has become a primary source of news for many, significantly impacting public opinion, political processes, and societal changes.

10. Corporate Responsibility and Social Awareness

Social media has given rise to increased corporate responsibility and social awareness. Brands are often held accountable by their audiences, leading to more ethical business practices and greater focus on social and environmental issues.

Conclusion

The importance of social media in today's economy cannot be over-stated. It has created new economic paradigms, redefined how businesses operate, and reshaped consumer behavior. As social media continues to evolve, its role in the economy will only grow more significant, offering unparalleled opportunities for innovation, growth, and global connectivity.

Facebook: Creating a Page or Profile

Setting up a Facebook profile or page is a crucial step in tapping into the platform's vast potential for communication, engagement, and monetization. Whether you're an individual looking to build a brand, a business aiming to expand your customer base, or a creator wanting to share content, Facebook offers various tools and features to help you achieve your goals. Here's an exhaustive guide on how to set up your Facebook profile or page:

1. Understanding the Difference Between a Profile and a Page

- **Profile**: A Facebook profile is a personal account. It's meant for individual use and represents a person. It's ideal for connecting with friends and family, sharing personal updates, and joining groups.

- **Page**: A Facebook Page is a public profile specifically created for businesses, brands, celebrities, causes, and other organizations. Unlike personal profiles, Pages can gain an unlimited number of followers.

2. Setting Up a Personal Profile

- **Step 1: Sign Up**

  - Visit Facebook.com and fill out the sign-up form with your name, email or mobile number, password, date of birth, and gender.

  - Click "Sign Up" to proceed.

- **Step 2: Profile Customization**

  - Upload a profile picture and cover photo that represents you or your personal brand.

  - Fill in your personal details like education, work, and interests in the "About" section.

- **Step 3: Privacy Settings**

  - Adjust your privacy settings from the settings menu to control who sees your posts, friend list, and profile information.

- **Step 4: Building Your Network**

○ Start by adding friends and joining groups that align
with your interests or industry.

3. Creating a Facebook Page

- **Step 1: Page Creation**

  ○ Log into your Facebook profile.

  ○ Go to the Create a Page section.

  ○ Choose a Page type: Business/Brand or Communi-
  ty/Public Figure.

  ○ Enter your Page name and category that describes your
  Page. Fill in the address and contact details if necessary.

- **Step 2: Page Customization**

  ○ Upload a profile picture and cover photo that reflect your
  brand or organization.

  ○ Complete the "About" section, providing details about
  your business or brand. This should include your website, a brief description, and other essential information.

- **Step 3: Page Settings and Roles**

  ○ In the Page settings, you can assign roles if you have a
  team. Roles include admin, editor, moderator, advertis-
  er, and analyst, each with different levels of access and
  control.

- **Step 4: Publishing Content**

  - Start creating and posting content relevant to your brand. This can include updates, photos, videos, events, and more.

  - Utilize Facebook's post scheduling feature to maintain a consistent posting schedule.

- **Step 5: Engagement and Growth**

  - Invite friends and contacts to like and follow your Page.

  - Engage with your audience by responding to comments and messages.

  - Consider using Facebook ads to reach a wider audience.

- **Step 6: Insights and Analytics**

  - Regularly check your Page insights to understand your audience better and see what content performs well.

- **Step 7: Continual Updating**

  - Keep your Page updated with fresh content and accurate information. Regular updates and engagement are key to growing your presence.

Conclusion

Setting up a Facebook profile or Page is just the beginning of your social media journey. The real work lies in consistently managing and optimizing your presence on the platform. For businesses and creators, a Facebook Page offers extensive tools and analytics to engage with audiences and monetize your presence. Personal profiles, while not meant for direct monetization, play a crucial role in networking and personal branding.

Instagram: Account Setup and Business Conversion

Setting Up Your Social Media Profiles

Instagram has emerged as a vital platform for brand building, content sharing, and monetization, especially for visually driven content. Whether you're a creator, business, or individual looking to expand your reach, Instagram offers a plethora of features to engage with a broad audience. Here's a comprehensive guide on setting up an Instagram account and converting it to a business profile:

1. Setting Up an Instagram Account

- **Step 1: Download and Install**

  - Download the Instagram app from the Apple App Store or Google Play Store.

  - Alternatively, you can visit the Instagram website for account creation.

- **Step 2: Sign Up**

  - Open the app or website and choose to sign up with your email address, phone number, or Facebook account.

  - Enter the required information, including name and password.

- **Step 3: Profile Customization**

  - Choose a username that reflects your identity or brand. It should be recognizable and easy to search

  - Upload a profile picture that represents you or your brand. This could be a headshot, logo, or another relevant image.

  - Fill in your bio with a brief, engaging description of yourself or your business. You can include hashtags and links.

- **Step 4: Exploring Instagram**

  - Start following other accounts, including peers, influencers, brands, and friends, to build your network.

○ Familiarize yourself with Instagram's interface: Feed, Stories, Reels, Explore, and Profile settings.

2. Converting to a Business Profile

- **Step 1: Switch to Business Profile**

  ○ Go to your profile and tap the hamburger icon (≡) in the top right corner.

  ○ Tap "Settings," then "Account."

  ○ Select "Switch to Professional Account," then choose "Business."

- **Step 2: Business Information**

  ○ Fill in your business details, including the category that best describes your business and contact information.

  ○ Connect your Instagram business profile to a Facebook Page associated with your business. This step is optional but recommended for full functionality.

- **Step 3: Profile Optimization for Business**

  ○ Optimize your bio with business-relevant information, including a clear description of what you offer, a call-to-action (CTA), and a link to your website or a landing page.

- Consider using Instagram's business tools like action buttons (e.g., Book, Contact, Shop) to facilitate customer interaction.

- **Step 4: Utilizing Business Features**

  - Explore Instagram Insights to understand your audience demographics, engagement rates, and content performance.

  - Use Instagram's advertising platform to promote posts and reach a larger, more targeted audience.

  - Leverage Instagram Shopping if you're selling products directly through the platform.

- **Step 5: Content Strategy for Business Accounts**

  - Develop a content strategy that aligns with your brand identity. This includes regular posts, Stories, and Reels.

  - Engage with your audience through comments, direct messages, and interactive stories.

- **Step 6: Regular Monitoring and Adjusting**

  - Continuously monitor your account's performance through insights.

  - Adjust your strategy based on what content performs best and audience feedback.

Conclusion

An Instagram account, particularly a business profile, is a powerful tool for building an online presence, engaging with audiences, and driving business goals. The key to success on Instagram lies in understanding the platform's features, creating visually appealing and engaging content, and actively engaging with your community. Regular analysis and adaptation of your strategy based on insights and trends are crucial for sustained growth and success.

TikTok: Starting Your Account

Setting Up Your Social Media Profiles

TikTok has rapidly grown into a highly influential social media platform, particularly known for its short-form video content that resonates with a younger audience. It's a powerful tool for creators looking to showcase their creativity, businesses aiming to tap into a younger demographic, and anyone interested in building a following through engaging video content. Here's a detailed guide to starting your account on TikTok:

1. Downloading and Installing the App

- **Step 1: Install TikTok**

    - Download the TikTok app from the Apple App Store or

Google Play Store.

- ○ TikTok can also be accessed via a web browser, but the app offers a fuller experience.

2. Creating a TikTok Account

- **Step 2: Sign Up**

  - ○ Open the app and sign up using your phone number, email address, or a linked social media account (e.g. , Facebook, Google).

  - ○ Set a strong password for your account.

- **Step 3: Profile Setup**

  - ○ Choose a username that is catchy, memorable, and reflective of you or your brand. It should be easy for others to find and recognize.

  - ○ Add a profile picture or video that represents you or your brand. This could be a logo, headshot, or any other image that captures the essence of your content.

- **Step 4: Bio and Personalization**

  - ○ Write a concise and engaging bio. Although TikTok bios are short, they are a great opportunity to make a first impression. You can include hashtags or links to other social media profiles.

  - ○ Explore the app settings to customize your privacy and

notification preferences.

3. Understanding TikTok's Interface and Features

- **Step 5: Navigating TikTok**

  - Familiarize yourself with TikTok's main interface, including the Home feed, Discover tab, Inbox, and Me (your profile).

  - Explore the types of content on your For You page and Following feed to understand popular trends and content styles.

4. Creating and Posting Your First TikTok

- **Step 6: Making a Video**

  - Tap the "+" icon to start creating a video.

  - Use TikTok's in-app camera or upload a video from your gallery.

  - Experiment with TikTok's editing tools, effects, filters, music, and text options to enhance your video.

- **Step 7: Posting Content**

  - Once you're happy with your video, write a catchy caption, include relevant hashtags, and choose a cover image.

- You can tag people, add a location, and control who can comment on your video before posting.

5. Engaging with the TikTok Community

- **Step 8: Interaction and Growth**

  - Start following other users and engage with their content through likes, comments, and shares.

  - Respond to comments on your videos to foster a community and encourage engagement.

6. Understanding TikTok Analytics

- **Step 9: Monitoring Performance**

  - As you post more content, monitor your TikTok analytics to understand your audience and what type of content resonates the most.

  - Use these insights to refine your content strategy and posting schedule.

Conclusion

Starting a TikTok account is just the beginning. The key to success on TikTok lies in understanding its unique culture and trends, creating original and engaging content, and actively participating in the community. Consistency, creativity, and engagement are crucial for building a presence and following on TikTok. Stay updated with the latest trends, experiment with different content types, and most importantly, have fun with the process!

Twitter: Building a Profile for Engagement

Setting Up Your Social Media Profiles

Twitter is a powerful platform known for its real-time content, brevity, and wide reach. It's particularly effective for engagement, networking, and building influence in various fields. Whether you're an individual looking to establish a personal brand, a professional aiming to network in your industry, or a business seeking to connect with customers, Twitter offers a unique space for these interactions. Here's a detailed guide on building a Twitter profile geared towards engagement:

1. Signing Up and Creating Your Account

- **Step 1: Sign Up**

    ○ Download the Twitter app from the Apple App Store or Google Play Store, or visit the Twitter website.

    ○ Create an account using your email address or phone number.

    ○ Choose a username (handle) that reflects your identity or brand. Twitter handles are unique and become a part of your Twitter URL (e.g., twitter.com/yourhandle).

- **Step 2: Profile Setup**

    ○ Add a profile picture that represents you or your brand effectively. This could be a headshot, logo, or any relevant image.

    ○ Create a header image that complements your profile picture and represents your brand or personality.

- **Step 3: Crafting Your Bio**

    ○ Write a compelling bio. Your bio has a 160-character limit, so make it concise yet informative. Include keywords relevant to your interests or business, and you can also add a link to your website or a landing page.

    ○ Utilize the location field to add your city or region, which can be useful for local networking.

2. Understanding Twitter's Interface and Features

- **Step 4: Navigating the Platform**

  - Familiarize yourself with the Twitter interface: Home feed, Explore, Notifications, and Messages.

  - Understand how to compose tweets, retweet, like, and reply to posts.

3. Building Your Network

- **Step 5: Following Relevant Accounts**

  - Start following other accounts, including influencers, businesses, news sources, and individuals in your field or area of interest.

  - Engage with their content by liking, retweeting, and replying to tweets.

- **Step 6: Your First Tweets**

  - Compose and share your first tweets. These could be introductory, sharing insights, or commenting on relevant topics.

  - Use hashtags strategically to increase the visibility of your tweets. Don't overuse them; focus on relevance and trending topics.

4. Engaging and Growing Your Audience

- **Step 7: Regular Posting and Engagement**

  ○ Tweet regularly but prioritize quality over quantity. Share updates, insights, images, videos, and links that provide value to your followers.

  ○ Engage with your audience by responding to comments and direct messages.

- **Step 8: Leveraging Twitter Tools**

  ○ Utilize Twitter lists to organize accounts you follow and curate content streams.

  ○ Consider using Twitter Spaces (live audio conversations) to engage with your audience in real-time.

5. Monitoring and Improving Your Engagement

- **Step 9: Using Analytics**

  ○ Monitor your Twitter analytics to understand your audience and what type of content resonates with them.

  ○ Adjust your content strategy based on engagement metrics and audience feedback.

Conclusion

Building a profile for engagement on Twitter requires a strategic approach that combines effective communication, regular engagement, and content that resonates with your intended audience. It's about establishing a voice and a presence that invites interaction and fosters relationships. Keep in mind that Twitter is a dynamic platform where trends and conversations change rapidly, so staying active, relevant, and responsive is key to building and maintaining engagement.

Understanding Platform Interfaces

Navigating the interfaces of different social media platforms is crucial for effective use and monetization. Each platform has its unique layout, features, and tools, designed to enhance user experience and engagement. Understanding these interfaces allows you to maximize the potential of each platform for your personal or business goals. Below is an overview of the interfaces of Facebook, Instagram, TikTok, and Twitter.

1. Facebook Interface

- **News Feed**: The central hub where you see updates from friends, Pages you follow, and ads. It's tailored based on your interactions.

- **Timeline/Profile**: Your personal space showing your posts, friends, photos, and personal information.

- **Pages**: For businesses and public figures to connect with followers. Features include posting updates, insights, and page management tools.

- **Groups**: Spaces for users with common interests. They can be public or private.

- **Marketplace**: A feature for buying and selling items locally.

- **Messenger**: Integrated messaging app for private and group chats.

- **Notifications**: Alerts for interactions like comments, likes, and new followers.

- **Explore**: Section to discover new content, pages, and groups based on your interests.

2. Instagram Interface

- **Home Feed**: Displays posts, Stories, and Reels from followed accounts and suggested content.

- **Explore Page**: A discovery tool showing content tailored to your interests, based on your interactions.

- **Reels**: Dedicated tab for short-form video content, similar to TikTok.

- **Activity**: Shows your interactions, like likes and comments on your posts.

- **Profile**: Displays your posts, bio, and user information. Includes options for editing your profile and settings.

- **Direct Messages (DMs)**: For private messaging with other users.

- **Stories**: For sharing temporary (24-hour) photos and video updates.

- **IGTV**: Long-form video content section, accessible from the main profile.

3. TikTok Interface

- **For You Page (FYP)**: The main feed showing a stream of videos from various creators, tailored to your interests.

- **Following**: A feed of videos from accounts you follow.

- **Discover**: Helps you find trending challenges, hashtags, and sounds.

- **Create (+ Button)**: For making and posting your videos.

- **Inbox**: Where you receive notifications about your account and interactions.

- **Me (Profile)**: Displays your videos, liked content (if public), and user information. Also includes settings.

4. Twitter Interface

- **Home Feed**: Shows tweets from accounts you follow, plus suggested content.

- **Explore**: Discover trending topics, hashtags, and popular tweets.

- **Notifications**: Alerts for interactions with your tweets or account.

- **Messages**: Private messaging area for direct conversations.

- **Profile**: Displays your tweets, retweets, media, and information. Includes edit options for your profile and settings.

- **Tweet Button**: Quick access button to compose new tweets.

- **Lists**: Curated groups of accounts you can create or follow.

- **More**: Access additional features like bookmarks, moments, and Twitter Spaces.

Conclusion

Each platform's interface is designed to optimize user experience and engagement. Understanding these interfaces is key to navigating the platforms efficiently, whether for personal use, content creation, or business purposes. Familiarizing yourself with each platform's unique features and layout will allow you to leverage their full potential in your social media strategy.

Basic Security and Privacy Settings

In the realm of social media, maintaining security and privacy is paramount. Each platform offers a range of settings to help you protect your personal information and control who sees your content. Understanding and correctly configuring these settings can significantly enhance your online safety and privacy. Here's a look at the basic security and privacy settings for Facebook, Instagram, TikTok, and Twitter:

1. Facebook Security and Privacy Settings

- **Account Security**

  - **Password**: Regularly update your password and ensure it's strong and unique.

- **Two-Factor Authentication (2FA)**: Enable 2FA for an added layer of security.

- **Login Alerts**: Set up alerts to notify you of unrecognized logins.

- **Privacy Settings**

  - **Profile Visibility**: Control who can see your posts, friend list, and profile information.

  - **Tagging**: Manage who can tag you in posts and how these tags appear on your timeline.

  - **Location Services**: Opt-in or opt-out of location tracking features.

  - **Ad Preferences**: Customize your ad preferences and data settings.

2. Instagram Security and Privacy Settings

- **Account Security**

  - **Password Strength**: Use a secure password and change it periodically.

  - **Two-Factor Authentication**: Activate 2FA via SMS or an authentication app.

  - **Login Activity**: Monitor your login activity and log out from unfamiliar devices.

- **Privacy Settings**

  - **Account Privacy**: Choose between a public or private account.

  - **Story and Post Controls**: Decide who can view and respond to your stories and posts.

  - **Comment Controls**: Filter out offensive comments and control who can comment.

  - **Activity Status**: Choose whether to show your activity status.

3. TikTok Security and Privacy Settings

- **Account Security**

  - **Password Management**: Use a strong password and update it regularly.

  - **2FA and Verification**: Enable verification methods for additional security.

  - **Security Alerts**: Set up alerts for new logins or changes to account settings.

- **Privacy Settings**

  - **Private Account**: Make your account private so only approved followers can see your content.

  - **Direct Messages**: Control who can send you messages.

- **Comment Filters**: Manage who can comment and customize comment filters.

- **Duet and Stitch Settings**: Control who can Duet or Stitch with your videos.

4. Twitter Security and Privacy Settings

- **Account Security**

  - **Password Security**: Regularly change your password to a strong, unique combination.

  - **Login Verification (2FA)**: Implement 2FA to secure your account further.

  - **Login History and Devices**: Regularly check your login history and review active sessions.

- **Privacy Settings**

  - **Tweet Privacy**: Choose if your tweets are public or protected.

  - **Tagging**: Control who can tag you in photos.

  - **Direct Messages**: Decide who can send you direct messages.

  - **Discoverability**: Control whether you can be found by your email or phone number.

Conclusion

Regularly reviewing and updating your security and privacy settings is essential in safeguarding your online presence. Each social media platform offers various options to customize these settings according to your comfort and privacy preferences. By taking these steps, you can enjoy a safer and more controlled social media experience.

Tips for a Strong Start: Profile Optimization

Optimizing your social media profiles is key to making a strong start on any platform. A well-optimized profile not only enhances your visibility but also helps in building credibility and attracting the right audience. Whether you're using Facebook, Instagram, TikTok, or Twitter, certain universal tips can significantly boost your profile's effectiveness. Here's a guide to optimizing your social media profiles for a strong start:

1. Clear and Recognizable Profile Picture

- Use a high-quality, clear profile picture that represents you or your brand effectively. This could be a headshot, a logo, or any image that captures the essence of your personal or business brand.

2. Compelling Bio/Description

- Craft a bio or description that succinctly conveys who you are, what you do, and what value you offer. Include relevant keywords and hashtags for better visibility. For businesses, incorporating a call-to-action (CTA) like a website link or a contact method is beneficial.

3. Consistent Branding Across Platforms

- Maintain consistency in your branding across all platforms. Use similar profile pictures, names, and aesthetic themes to create a recognizable and coherent brand image.

4. Engaging Cover/Header Images

- Utilize cover or header images to complement your profile picture. This space can be used for branding purposes, to showcase your work, or to convey key information about your brand or personality.

5. Utilizing the 'About' Sections Effectively

- Fill out all the fields in the 'About' section, including location, contact information, and website links. For businesses, include operating hours and services offered.

6. Strategic Use of Keywords and Hashtags

- Incorporate relevant keywords and hashtags in your profile description and content. This improves searchability and helps in reaching the right audience.

7. Linking Other Social Media Accounts

- If applicable, link your other social media accounts or relevant webpages. This encourages cross-platform engagement and gives your audience a holistic view of your online presence.

8. Regular Content Updates

- Start by posting content regularly. Consistency is key in building an audience. Plan your content in advance and maintain a content calendar to stay organized.

9. Engaging with Your Audience Early On

- Engage with your audience through comments, messages, and likes. Building a rapport with your followers can encourage loyalty and increase engagement.

10. Monitoring and Adjusting Based on Analytics

- Utilize platform analytics to monitor the performance of your profile and content. Adjust your strategy based on what resonates best with your audience.

Conclusion

A strong start on social media can set the foundation for future growth and engagement. By optimizing your profiles, you not only make a great first impression but also ensure that your social media efforts align with your personal or business goals. Remember, social media is an evolving space, so it's important to stay adaptable and keep updating your strategy as needed.

Facebook: Features, and Monetization Opportunities

F acebook, with its vast user base and comprehensive features, offers numerous opportunities for monetization. From businesses to individual creators, the platform provides various tools and avenues to generate revenue and build brand presence. Understanding these features and how they can be leveraged for monetization is key to succeeding on Facebook. Here's an overview:

1. Facebook Pages

- **Functionality**: Enables businesses, public figures, organizations, and other entities to create a public presence on Facebook.

- **Monetization**: Through sponsored content, selling products via Facebook Shop, hosting paid online events, and fan subscriptions.

2. Facebook Marketplace

- **Functionality**: A platform for buying and selling items within your local community or from businesses.

- **Monetization**: Ideal for individuals and businesses to sell products directly to consumers.

3. Facebook Groups

- **Functionality**: Groups are for users to connect over shared interests. They can be public or private.

- **Monetization**: While direct monetization is limited, groups are excellent for building a community around a brand or niche, which can indirectly lead to monetization opportunities.

4. Facebook Ads

- **Functionality**: Allows businesses to create targeted ads to reach a specific audience.

- **Monetization**: Effective for promoting products, services, or content, leading to increased sales or traffic.

5. Facebook Live

- **Functionality**: Real-time video broadcasting feature.

- **Monetization**: Through audience support in the form of Stars (virtual goods that fans can buy to support creators during live videos).

6. Affiliate Marketing

- **Functionality**: Promoting products or services and earning a commission for each sale or referral.

- **Monetization**: By sharing affiliate links in posts, videos, or within a Facebook group.

7. Influencer Partnerships

- **Functionality**: Collaboration with brands for sponsored content.

- **Monetization**: By creating sponsored posts, videos, or stories in partnership with brands.

8. Facebook Watch and Videos

- **Functionality**: A platform for video content where users can discover, watch, and share videos.

- **Monetization**: Through ad breaks in videos, offering a share of the ad revenue to the creators.

9. Facebook Instant Articles

- **Functionality**: A feature for publishers to create fast, interactive articles on Facebook.

- **Monetization**: Publishers can earn money from ads placed in their articles.

10. Selling Digital Products or Services

- **Functionality**: Promoting and selling digital products like courses, ebooks, or digital art.

- **Monetization**: Through direct sales on the platform or linking to an external website or online store.

Conclusion

Facebook's diverse features offer a wide array of monetization opportunities. The key to successful monetization on Facebook lies in understanding the platform's algorithms, leveraging its vast network, and engaging effectively with your audience. Whether it's through direct sales, advertising, content creation, or partnerships, Facebook provides a fertile ground for various monetization strategies. Regularly updating your approach and staying informed about new features and trends is crucial for sustained success on the platform.

Instagram: Leveraging Visual Content, Features, and Monetization Opportunities

Instagram, known for its strong focus on visual content, offers a plethora of features that can be leveraged for both engagement and monetization. This platform is particularly beneficial for brands, influencers, and creators who thrive on visually appealing content. Understanding how to use these features effectively can lead to significant monetization opportunities. Here's a comprehensive overview:

1. Instagram Posts and Stories

- **Functionality**: Share photos and short videos on your feed, and ephemeral content through Stories.

- **Monetization Opportunities**: Sponsored posts, branded content, and product placement can be used to monetize regular posts and Stories.

2. Instagram Reels

- **Functionality**: Similar to TikTok, Reels allows users to create and share short, engaging video content.

- **Monetization Opportunities**: Engaging with trends and viral content on Reels can attract brand partnerships and sponsorships.

3. Instagram Live

- **Functionality**: Real-time video streaming to engage with followers.

- **Monetization Opportunities**: During live streams, creators can promote products, services, or partner with brands for live demonstrations or Q&A sessions.

4. Instagram IGTV

- **Functionality**: Platform for sharing longer-form video content.

- **Monetization Opportunities**: Monetization through ads in IGTV videos (where available), and by creating sponsored content or product reviews.

5. Instagram Shopping

- **Functionality**: Allows businesses to create an online storefront directly on Instagram.

- **Monetization Opportunities**: Direct selling of products through posts, Stories, and the dedicated Shop tab.

6. Affiliate Marketing

- **Functionality**: Promoting products or services and earning a commission for sales made through affiliate links.

- **Monetization Opportunities**: Share affiliate links in posts, Stories, or bio, particularly effective with lifestyle and fashion content.

7. Sponsored Content and Brand Collaborations

- **Functionality**: Partnering with brands to create content that promotes their products or services.

- **Monetization Opportunities**: Paid partnerships with

brands, where creators are compensated for featuring products in their content.

8. Instagram Ads

- **Functionality**: Paid advertising feature to reach a wider audience.

- **Monetization Opportunities**: Businesses and creators can use ads to promote their products, services, or content to a targeted audience.

9. Influencer Marketing

- **Functionality**: Influencers leverage their follower base to promote brands or products.

- **Monetization Opportunities**: Paid promotions, brand ambassadorships, and sponsored content deals.

10. Selling Digital Products or Services

- **Functionality**: Promoting services like photography, consulting, or digital products like e-books and courses.

- **Monetization Opportunities**: Direct sales through Instagram or linking to an external website where transactions can occur.

Conclusion

Instagram's visually driven platform is a goldmine for those looking to monetize their presence online. The key is to create visually appealing, engaging content that resonates with your audience while effectively leveraging the platform's features for exposure and revenue generation. Staying updated with the latest trends, engaging with your audience, and consistently delivering high-quality content are essential strategies for successful monetization on Instagram.

TikTok: Capitalizing on Trends and Viral Content, Features, and Monetization Opportunities

TikTok has become a hub for short-form video content, known for its viral trends, creative expression, and a highly engaged user base. The platform offers unique features and monetization opportunities, especially for content creators who can capitalize on its trend-driven environment. Understanding these aspects is key to leveraging TikTok for personal, brand, or business growth. Here's an in-depth look at the features and monetization opportunities on TikTok:

1. Viral Content and Trend Participation

- **Functionality**: TikTok thrives on trending hashtags, sounds, and challenges.

- **Monetization Opportunities**: Engaging with popular trends can increase visibility and attract brand attention for potential partnerships or sponsorships.

2. TikTok Creator Fund

- **Functionality**: A monetization program that pays eligible creators for engaging content.

- **Monetization Opportunities**: Earn money directly from TikTok based on the performance and engagement of your videos.

3. TikTok Live

- **Functionality**: Live streaming feature that allows real-time interaction with followers.

- **Monetization Opportunities**: Receive gifts from viewers that can be converted into money. Also, a platform for promoting products or services during the stream.

4. TikTok Ads

- **Functionality**: A platform for businesses to create ads that appear in between user videos.

- **Monetization Opportunities**: For brands and businesses, TikTok ads can drive traffic to websites or online stores, increasing sales or conversions.

5. Brand Partnerships

- **Functionality**: Collaborating with brands for sponsored content.

- **Monetization Opportunities**: Paid partnerships where creators make branded content that features products or services.

6. Affiliate Marketing

- **Functionality**: Promoting products or services through affiliate links.

- **Monetization Opportunities**: Earn commissions by including affiliate links in video descriptions or your TikTok bio.

7. TikTok's Creator Marketplace

- **Functionality**: An official platform connecting brands with TikTok creators for marketing collaborations.

- **Monetization Opportunities**: Facilitates partnerships and sponsorships between creators and brands.

8. Selling Merchandise

- **Functionality**: Promoting and selling personal merchandise or products.

- **Monetization Opportunities**: Direct sales through linking to external websites where followers can purchase products.

9. In-App E-Commerce Integration

- **Functionality**: TikTok is experimenting with in-app shopping features.

- **Monetization Opportunities**: Directly sell products through TikTok, making it easier for users to shop without leaving the app.

10. Content Creation for Others

- **Functionality**: Offering content creation services to brands and businesses.

- **Monetization Opportunities**: Paid contracts or freelance work creating TikTok content for clients.

Conclusion

TikTok offers a dynamic and unique platform for monetization, particularly suited for those who excel at creating short, engaging video content. The key to success on TikTok lies in understanding its trend-centric culture, engaging actively with the community, and creatively leveraging its features to build a following and attract monetization opportunities. Staying adaptable, regularly experimenting with new content types, and maintaining an authentic voice are crucial to thriving on TikTok.

Twitter: Monetizing Through Engagement and Influence, Features, and Monetization Opportunities

Twitter, known for its concise content and real-time communication, offers unique opportunities for monetization, particularly for those who can harness its power of engagement and influence.

Unlike platforms primarily driven by visual content, Twitter relies on quick, impactful messages and interactions. Understanding how to utilize its features for monetization requires a strategic approach. Here's a detailed exploration of Twitter's features and the monetization opportunities they present:

1. Sponsored Tweets and Brand Partnerships

- **Functionality**: Creating content that includes promotional material for brands.

- **Monetization Opportunities**: Earning income through sponsored content deals with brands, where you get paid to tweet about their products or services.

2. Affiliate Marketing

- **Functionality**: Sharing affiliate links in your tweets.

- **Monetization Opportunities**: Earning commissions for sales made through affiliate links posted in your tweets.

3. Twitter Ads

- **Functionality**: A platform for creating targeted advertisements.

- **Monetization Opportunities**: For businesses and content creators, Twitter ads can increase reach and drive traffic to monetized websites or online stores.

4. Building and Selling a Twitter Profile

- **Functionality**: Growing a Twitter account with a substantial follower base.

- **Monetization Opportunities**: Selling the account to businesses or individuals looking for a pre-established audience (Note: This practice may be against Twitter's terms of service and is often frowned upon).

5. Twitter Spaces

- **Functionality**: Hosting live audio conversations on various topics.

- **Monetization Opportunities**: Promoting products or services during the conversation, or collaborating with brands for sponsored Spaces.

6. Content Creation for Other Brands or Individuals

- **Functionality**: Creating Twitter content for third parties.

- **Monetization Opportunities**: Offering services as a Twitter content strategist or manager for brands, businesses, or influencers.

7. Tip Jar and Super Follows

- **Functionality**: Features that allow users to monetize their Twitter audience directly.

- **Monetization Opportunities**:

    ○ **Tip Jar**: Enables followers to send money directly to their favorite creators.

    ○ **Super Follows**: Allows creators to charge for access to additional, exclusive content.

8. Selling Digital Products or Services

- **Functionality**: Promoting and selling digital products like e-books, courses, or services like consulting.

- **Monetization Opportunities**: Direct sales through linking to external websites where transactions can take place.

9. Using Twitter to Drive Traffic

- **Functionality**: Leveraging Twitter to drive followers to monetized blogs, YouTube channels, or other social media platforms.

- **Monetization Opportunities**: Increasing revenue on other platforms through increased traffic from Twitter.

10. Hosting Twitter Chats and Events

- **Functionality**: Organizing scheduled discussions or events around specific hashtags.

- **Monetization Opportunities**: Sponsored events or collaborations with brands relevant to the chat topic.

Conclusion

Twitter's monetization potential lies in the ability to create influential content, engage with a dedicated audience, and leverage the platform's features for various marketing and promotional activities. Success on Twitter is often tied to how well one can communicate a message within its character limit and engage with real-time trends and conversations. For those who can navigate its unique environment effectively, Twitter offers diverse ways to monetize their presence and influence.

Building Your Presence

Identifying Your Niche

1. **Assess Your Interests and Strengths**:

   - Reflect on what you are passionate about. This could be a specific genre in literature, a topic you're knowledgeable about, or a unique perspective you hold.

   - Consider your skills and strengths. What do you do well? Are there subjects or activities where you consistently excel?

   - Think about your unique experiences and how they could inform your niche. Personal stories or specialized knowledge can be a powerful differentiator.

2. **Research the Market**:

   - Investigate current trends in the area you're interested in.

Are there emerging topics that align with your interests?

- Analyze the competition. See what others in your potential niche are doing. What can you offer that's different or better?

- Consider the demand. Is there a readership or audience for your niche? Use tools like Google Trends, social media insights, or publishing industry reports to gauge interest levels.

3. **Identify Your Target Audience**:

- Define who your ideal readers or viewers are. Consider demographics like age, gender, interests, and geographical location.

- Understand the needs and preferences of your audience. What do they look for in books or content? What challenges or questions do they have that you can address?

4. **Test Your Ideas**:

- Experiment with different themes or topics within your area of interest. This could be through blog posts, short stories, social media content, or even informal discussions with potential readers.

- Gather feedback. Pay attention to what resonates with your audience and what doesn't.

5. **Refine Your Focus**:

- Based on your research and testing, narrow down your

niche. It should be specific enough to set you apart but broad enough to sustain your creative output and interest over time.

- Develop a unique angle or approach. How will you tackle your chosen niche differently than others?

6. **Build Your Presence**:

- Start creating content consistently within your niche. Whether it's writing books, articles, or social media posts, regular output helps establish your presence.

- Network with others in your field. Attend events, join online communities, and connect with fellow authors or creators.

- Utilize multiple platforms. Depending on your niche, consider a mix of blogging, social media, videos, podcasts, or public speaking to reach your audience.

7. **Stay Flexible and Open to Evolution**:

- Be prepared to adapt your niche as trends change and as you gain more insight into what works and what doesn't.

- Continuously learn and evolve. Stay updated with new developments in your field and be open to incorporating new ideas into your work.

Remember, finding your niche is often an iterative process. It's about combining your passion and expertise with what the market needs or is interested in. As you grow and evolve, so too might your niche. The key is to remain authentic to your interests and strengths while being responsive to your audience.

Content Creation Strategies

Creating compelling content is central to building and maintaining a strong presence on social media. It's not just about posting frequently; it's about delivering value in a way that resonates with your audience. Here are key strategies for creating content that can help elevate your presence on platforms like Facebook, Instagram, TikTok, and Twitter:

Understand Your Audience

- **Research Your Audience**: Understand their interests, needs, and behaviors. Use platform analytics to gain insights into their demographics and preferences.

- **Tailor Your Content**: Create content that addresses your audience's interests, challenges, and questions.

2. Develop a Consistent Theme and Style

- **Consistency in Aesthetics**: Maintain a consistent color scheme, tone, and style that reflects your brand or personal identity.

- **Thematic Content**: Develop content themes or series that align with your brand and appeal to your audience.

3. Leverage Different Content Formats

- **Diversify Your Content**: Use a mix of text, images, videos, and interactive content like polls and quizzes.

- **Platform-Specific Formats**: Adapt to each platform's strengths (e.g., Stories on Instagram, short-form videos on TikTok, concise tweets on Twitter).

4. Embrace Storytelling

- **Narrative Content**: Share stories that engage and connect with your audience on an emotional level.

- **Personal Touch**: Include personal experiences and insights to make your content more relatable.

5. Stay Current with Trends

- **Monitor Trends**: Keep up with current trends and topics relevant to your niche.

- **Incorporate Trending Topics**: Integrate popular and trending themes creatively into your content.

6. Utilize Visuals Effectively

- **High-Quality Visuals**: Use high-quality images and videos to make your content more engaging.

- **Visual Branding**: Ensure your visuals are on-brand and reinforce your identity.

7. Experiment with Interactive Content

- **Engage Your Audience**: Create polls, quizzes, and ask-me-anything (AMA) sessions to interact with your audience.

- **User-Generated Content**: Encourage your audience to share their own content related to your brand or niche.

8. Schedule and Plan Content

- **Content Calendar**: Develop a content calendar to plan and schedule your posts.

- **Consistent Posting**: Maintain a consistent posting schedule to keep your audience engaged.

9. SEO Optimization

- **Keywords and Hashtags**: Use relevant keywords and hashtags to improve visibility and discoverability.

- **Optimize for Search**: For platforms like YouTube and blog posts, optimize titles, descriptions, and tags for search engines.

10. Analyze and Adapt

- **Monitor Performance**: Regularly review your content's performance through platform analytics.

- **Adapt Strategies**: Be prepared to adjust your content strategy based on what works best for your audience.

Conclusion

Effective content creation is a dynamic process that requires understanding your audience, staying relevant, and continuously experimenting and adapting. By employing these strategies, you can create content that not only attracts but also retains a dedicated following, thereby strengthening your social media presence.

Growing Your Audience

Growing your audience on social media is a critical step in establishing a strong online presence. Whether you're a brand, influencer, or individual, expanding your reach requires a mix of strategic planning, engagement, and content optimization. Here's a comprehensive approach to increasing your follower base across platforms like Facebook, Instagram, TikTok, and Twitter:

1. Understand and Define Your Target Audience

- **Audience Analysis**: Identify the demographics, interests, and behaviors of your ideal audience.

- **Targeted Content**: Create content that resonates specifically with the audience you want to attract.

2. Engage with Similar Communities

- **Join Groups and Forums**: Participate in relevant groups, forums, and online communities.

- **Engagement**: Actively engage in discussions, offer value, and share your insights.

3. Collaborate with Others

- **Partnerships**: Collaborate with other creators, influencers, or brands in your niche.

- **Cross-Promotion**: Engage in cross-promotional activities to tap into each other's audiences.

4. Use Hashtags Effectively

- **Relevant Hashtags**: Use hashtags that are relevant to your content and niche.

- **Hashtag Research**: Find out which hashtags are popular and trending in your area of interest.

5. Consistency in Posting

- **Regular Content**: Post content regularly to keep your audience engaged and attract new followers.

- **Consistent Schedule**: Maintain a consistent posting schedule so your audience knows when to expect new content.

6. Leverage Trends and Viral Content

- **Trending Topics**: Create content around trending topics or viral challenges to gain visibility.

- **Adapt Trends**: Adapt trends to fit your niche and brand voice.

7. Optimize Your Profile and Bio

- **Profile Optimization**: Ensure your social media profiles are complete, professional, and align with your brand.

- **Bio and Links**: Use your bio to convey your brand message and include links to your website or other social profiles.

8. High-Quality and Diverse Content

- **Content Quality**: Ensure your content is high-quality, informative, and visually appealing.

- **Content Variety**: Mix up your content types (images, videos, blogs) to keep your audience engaged.

9. Paid Promotion and Advertising

- **Social Media Ads**: Invest in social media advertising to reach a larger audience.

- **Targeted Campaigns**: Create targeted ad campaigns to reach potential followers who fit your audience profile.

10. Engage with Your Followers

- **Audience Interaction**: Respond to comments, messages, and engage with your followers' content.

- **Community Building**: Foster a sense of community by encouraging dialogue and interaction among your followers.

11. Monitor Analytics and Adjust Strategy

- **Analyze Performance**: Use social media analytics to track the growth and engagement of your audience.

- **Iterative Approach**: Continuously refine your strategy based on analytics and feedback.

Conclusion

Growing your audience on social media is a multifaceted process that involves understanding your target audience, creating engaging content, and actively participating in the social media community. Combining these strategies with regular analysis and adaptation can lead to sustained growth and a strong online presence.

Engagement: Interacting with Followers

Engaging with your followers is a fundamental aspect of building and maintaining a strong presence on social media. Interaction not only helps in fostering a loyal community but also boosts the visibility and reach of your content. Here are key strategies for effectively interacting with followers on platforms like Facebook, Instagram, TikTok, and Twitter:

1. Prompt and Personalized Responses

- **Respond to Comments**: Make it a habit to respond to comments on your posts promptly. Personalized responses rather than generic replies can make a big difference.

- **Engage in Conversations**: Don't just respond; engage in meaningful conversations. Ask follow-up questions or share your thoughts to deepen the interaction.

2. Utilize Direct Messages

- **Personal Interaction**: Use direct messages (DMs) for more personalized interaction with your followers.

- **Customer Service**: Address queries or concerns via DMs, which can be crucial for businesses.

3. Acknowledge and Share User-Generated Content

- **Repost and Share**: Share user-generated content related to your brand or content. This could be stories, posts, or mentions.

- **Give Credit**: Always give credit to the original poster when you share their content.

4. Host Q&A Sessions and AMAs

- **Interactive Sessions**: Regularly host question-and-answer sessions or "Ask Me Anything" (AMA) to engage with your audience.

- **Use Platform Features**: Utilize features like Instagram Stories' question sticker or Twitter threads for these sessions.

5. Conduct Polls and Surveys

- **Engagement Tools**: Use polls and surveys to engage your audience and gather feedback.

- **Content Ideas**: Polls can also be a great way to get ideas for future content.

6. Comment and Engage on Followers' Posts

- **Show Interest**: Make an effort to comment on your followers' posts. This shows that you value and appreciate your community.

- **Build Relationships**: Regular engagement helps in building stronger relationships with your audience.

7. Go Live Regularly

- **Live Interactions**: Use live streaming features to interact with your audience in real time.

- **Real-Time Feedback**: Live sessions are great for immediate feedback and spontaneous interaction.

8. Create Community Spaces

- **Groups and Forums**: Create or participate in Facebook groups, Twitter chats, or other online communities relevant to your niche.

- **Encourage Discussion**: Use these spaces to encourage discussions and community building.

9. Show Appreciation

- **Thank Your Followers**: Regularly express gratitude to your followers for their support and engagement.

- **Special Mentions**: Acknowledge loyal followers or highlight standout comments and interactions.

10. Stay Authentic and Genuine

- **Be Yourself**: Maintain authenticity in your interactions. Genuine engagement is more valued than forced or scripted interaction.

Conclusion

Effective engagement with followers is about creating a sense of community and belonging. It involves being responsive, showing appreciation, and genuinely interacting with your audience. This not only nurtures your existing follower base but also attracts new followers, contributing to the overall growth and vitality of your social media presence.

Monetization Strategies

Sponsored Content and Partnerships

In the realm of social media, sponsored content and partnerships represent a significant avenue for monetization. These strategies involve collaborating with brands or other entities to promote products, services, or campaigns. Here's a detailed look at how you can effectively leverage sponsored content and partnerships across various social media platforms:

1. Understanding Sponsored Content

- **Definition**: Sponsored content is any material (posts, videos, stories) created to promote a brand or its products, for which the creator is compensated.

- **Transparency**: Always disclose sponsored content to your audience, adhering to the guidelines set by the platform and regulatory authorities (like the FTC in the USA).

2. Identifying Potential Partnerships

- **Brand Alignment**: Seek partnerships with brands that align with your niche, values, and audience interests.

- **Outreach**: Proactively reach out to brands or wait for them to approach you. Utilize platforms like LinkedIn or specialized influencer marketing platforms for networking.

3. Creating Engaging Sponsored Content

- **Authenticity**: Ensure the content fits naturally within your usual content style to maintain authenticity.

- **Creativity**: Use creative and unique approaches to showcase the product or service, rather than just a straightforward promotion.

4. Leveraging Different Platforms

- **Instagram**: Ideal for visual content like sponsored posts, stories, and reels showcasing products.

- **Facebook**: Utilize posts, stories, and live features for sponsored content. Facebook groups can also be a platform for partnerships.

- **TikTok**: Create engaging sponsored videos that align with TikTok's dynamic and creative nature.

- **Twitter**: Use tweets, threads, or Twitter Spaces for promoting sponsored content in a more conversational and direct manner.

5. Negotiating Terms and Compensation

- **Rates**: Determine your rates based on factors like your follower count, engagement rate, and the extent of content creation required.

- **Contract**: Always have a clear contract outlining the deliverables, compensation, content rights, and any other obligations.

6. Measuring Success of Sponsored Campaigns

- **Analytics**: Utilize platform analytics to measure the performance of sponsored content.

- **Reporting**: Provide comprehensive reports to the sponsoring brand, including engagement metrics and audience feedback.

7. Building Long-Term Relationships with Brands

- **Consistent Performance**: Deliver high-quality content consistently to build trust with brands.

- **Open Communication**: Maintain clear and open communication with your brand partners for feedback and improvement.

8. Diversifying Sponsorship Opportunities

- **Multiple Brands**: Collaborate with various brands to diversify your monetization streams.

- **Different Formats**: Explore different content formats and promotional strategies to keep your sponsored content fresh and engaging.

Conclusion

Sponsored content and partnerships offer a lucrative way to monetize your social media presence. The key is to balance promotional content with your regular content, ensuring authenticity and audience trust. Building a strong, engaged following and maintaining a clear niche can make you an attractive partner for brands, leading to successful and profitable collaborations.

Affiliate Marketing

Affiliate marketing is a popular monetization strategy in the realm of social media. It involves promoting products or services and earning a commission for each sale or referral made through your unique affiliate link. This approach is advantageous as it doesn't require you to create a product; instead, you can earn by promoting existing products. Here's how to effectively use affiliate marketing across different social media platforms:

1. Understanding Affiliate Marketing

- **Basics**: Sign up for affiliate programs where companies offer commissions for promoting their products or services.

- **Affiliate Links**: You'll receive unique links tracking sales or actions generated from your promotions.

2. Choosing the Right Products or Services

- **Relevance**: Select products that align with your niche and are likely to interest your audience.

- **Quality**: Choose reputable products or services to maintain trust with your audience.

3. Integrating Affiliate Links into Your Content

- **Organic Integration**: Embed affiliate links in your content naturally. This could be through product reviews, tutorials, or recommendation lists.

- **Disclosures**: Always disclose affiliate links to your audience, adhering to transparency and ethical standards.

4. Platform-Specific Strategies

- **Instagram**: Use affiliate links in your bio, stories (swipe-up feature, if available), and post descriptions.

- **Facebook**: Share affiliate links in posts, your page, or relevant Facebook groups (if allowed).

- **TikTok**: While direct linking in posts isn't possible, you can direct viewers to the link in your bio or use TikTok's bio link feature.

- **Twitter**: Tweet about your experiences with the products and include your affiliate links.

5. Creating Engaging Content Around Products

- **Value-Driven Content**: Provide valuable information in your content, such as how-to guides, product benefits, and personal experiences.

- **Visual Content**: For platforms like Instagram and Tik-Tok, use visually appealing content like images and videos to showcase the products.

6. Tracking and Analyzing Performance

- **Analytics Tools**: Use analytics tools provided by the affiliate program to track the performance of your links.

- **Adjust Strategies**: Based on analytics, adjust your approach to improve engagement and conversions.

7. Building Trust with Your Audience

- **Honest Reviews**: Offer honest opinions about the products. Trust is key in affiliate marketing.

- **Engagement**: Respond to questions or comments about the products you are promoting.

8. Continuous Learning and Adaptation

- **Market Trends**: Stay updated with market trends and adjust your affiliate marketing strategies accordingly.

- **Diversify**: Don't rely on a single product or service; diversify your affiliate promotions to mitigate risks.

Conclusion

Affiliate marketing can be a lucrative way to monetize your social media presence, provided you approach it strategically. It's important to choose products that align with your niche, integrate affiliate links organically into your content, and maintain transparency and trust with your audience. Regularly analyzing your performance and adapting your strategy is key to maximizing your affiliate marketing success.

Selling Products or Services

Selling products or services directly through social media platforms is an effective way to monetize your online presence. With the growing integration of e-commerce features across social media, there are ample opportunities for businesses, creators, and influencers to generate revenue. Here's a guide to effectively selling products or services on various social media platforms:

1. Identifying What to Sell

- **Products**: This could range from physical goods like apparel and crafts to digital products like ebooks, courses, or software.

- **Services**: Offer services aligned with your expertise, such as consulting, coaching, design work, or content creation.

2. Utilizing Social Media Platforms

- **Instagram**: Leverage Instagram Shopping to tag products in posts and stories, and use the Shop tab on your profile.

- **Facebook**: Utilize Facebook Marketplace and Shops to sell products directly through your Facebook Page.

- **TikTok**: While direct selling features are limited, use TikTok to showcase products or services and direct traffic to your website.

- **Twitter**: Use tweets to promote your products or services, linking back to your website or online store.

3. Creating a Seamless Buying Experience

- **Integrated Shopping Features**: Utilize in-app shopping features where available for a seamless customer experience.

- **Clear CTA**: Include clear calls-to-action (CTA) in your posts, guiding followers on how to make a purchase.

4. Showcasing Your Products/Services

- **High-Quality Visuals**: Use high-quality images and videos to showcase your products.

- **Lifestyle Content**: Create content that shows your products or services in use, highlighting their benefits and features.

5. Leveraging Content Marketing

- **Educational Content**: Provide value through how-to guides, tutorials, or informative content related to your products/services.

- **Storytelling**: Use storytelling to connect with your audience and humanize your brand.

6. Customer Engagement and Service

- **Respond to Inquiries**: Promptly answer questions and engage with potential customers in comments or direct messages.

- **Feedback**: Encourage and share customer feedback and testimonials.

7. Promotions and Offers

- **Exclusive Deals**: Offer exclusive discounts or promotions to your social media followers.

- **Limited Time Offers**: Create urgency with limited-time offers or flash sales.

8. Analytics and Optimization

- **Track Performance**: Use social media analytics to track the performance of your sales-related posts and campaigns.

- **Optimize Strategy**: Continuously refine your approach based on performance data and customer feedback.

9. Building a Community

- **Engage Your Followers**: Build a community around your brand by engaging regularly and creating interactive content.

- **Brand Ambassadors**: Encourage satisfied customers to become brand ambassadors.

Conclusion

Selling products or services on social media requires a combination of strategic promotion, engaging content, and excellent customer service. By understanding the unique aspects of each platform and tailoring your approach, you can effectively reach and sell to your audience. Remember, trust and transparency are key, so always strive to maintain an authentic and customer-centric approach.

Advertisements and Promoted Posts

Advertisements and promoted posts on social media are powerful tools for monetization, especially for businesses, influencers, and content creators. These methods involve paying the social media platform to boost the visibility of your content to a wider or more targeted audience. Here's how to effectively utilize advertisements and promoted posts:

1. Understanding Advertisements on Social Media

- **Basics**: Ads on social media can take various forms, such as in-feed static posts, videos, stories, or banner ads.

- **Targeting**: One of the key strengths of social media ads is the ability to target specific demographics, interests, and behaviors.

2. Creating Effective Ads

- **Engaging Content**: Develop visually appealing and engaging content for your ads. Use high-quality images or videos and compelling copy.

- **Clear Call-to-Action (CTA)**: Include a clear CTA in your ads, directing viewers on what action to take next.

3. Using Promoted Posts

- **Promoting Existing Content**: Promoted posts are typically regular posts that you pay to promote to a wider audience. Choose posts that have performed well organically.

- **Objective**: Understand the objective of the promotion, whether it's brand awareness, lead generation, or driving traffic to a website.

4. Platform-Specific Strategies

- **Facebook and Instagram**: Leverage Facebook's Ads Manager for detailed targeting options. Use carousel ads, video ads, or sponsored stories.

- **Twitter**: Utilize promoted tweets to reach a broader audience. Twitter also offers targeting options based on interests and keywords.

- **LinkedIn**: Ideal for B2B advertisements. Use sponsored content, sponsored InMail, or text ads.

- **TikTok**: Although newer to the advertising game, TikTok offers unique ad formats like branded challenges and in-feed videos.

5. Budgeting and Bidding

- **Budget**: Set a clear budget for your ad campaigns. Social media platforms offer flexible budgeting options, from daily to lifetime budgets.

- **Bidding Strategy**: Understand the bidding process, whether it's cost per click (CPC), cost per impression (CPM), or cost per action (CPA).

6. Tracking and Analytics

- **Performance Metrics**: Use the platform's analytics tools to track the performance of your ads and promoted posts.

- **Adjustments**: Be prepared to make adjustments to your campaigns based on performance data.

7. A/B Testing

- **Experimentation**: Conduct A/B testing with different ad formats, copy, images, and targeting to see what works best.

- **Optimization**: Use the insights from A/B testing to optimize future campaigns.

8. Compliance and Best Practices

- **Ad Policies**: Adhere to the specific advertising policies of each social media platform.

- **Relevance and Quality**: Ensure your ads are relevant to your target audience and maintain a high standard of quality.

Conclusion

Advertisements and promoted posts are effective ways to reach a larger audience, increase brand exposure, and drive specific actions. The key to success lies in creating compelling content, targeting the right audience, and continuously analyzing and adjusting your strategy based on performance metrics. With the right approach, ads and promotions can significantly contribute to your social media monetization efforts.

Leveraging Analytics and Tools

Understanding Analytics
Simplified Guide to Social Media Analytics

Social media analytics are crucial for understanding the performance of your content and the behavior of your audience. These analytics provide insights that can help you optimize your strategies for better engagement and monetization. Here's a comprehensive yet straightforward explanation of social media analytics:

1. Key Metrics Explained

- **Reach**: The total number of unique users who have seen your content. It indicates the potential audience size.

- **Impressions**: The number of times your content was displayed, regardless of whether it was clicked or not.

- **Engagement**: Includes likes, comments, shares, and clicks.

High engagement rates usually indicate content resonance.

- **Engagement Rate**: A metric that shows the percentage of people who engaged with your content out of those who saw it.

- **Followers Growth**: The rate at which your follower count is increasing.

- **Click-Through Rate (CTR)**: The percentage of users who clicked on a link in your post out of the total viewers.

- **Conversion Rate**: The percentage of users who took a desired action (like making a purchase) after clicking on a link in your post.

2. Analyzing Audience Demographics

- **Demographic Data**: Includes age, gender, location, and language of your audience. This helps in tailoring content to the audience's preferences.

- **Behavior Patterns**: Look at when your audience is most active and their interaction patterns to optimize posting times and content types.

3. Content Performance Analysis

- **Popular Content**: Identify which types of content (videos, images, text posts) perform best in terms of engagement and reach.

- **Post Timing**: Determine the best times and days to post based on when your content receives the most engagement.

4. Tools for Analytics

- **Built-in Analytics Tools**: Platforms like Facebook Insights, Instagram Insights, Twitter Analytics, and TikTok Analytics offer a wealth of data.

- **Third-Party Tools**: Tools like Google Analytics, Hootsuite, and Sprout Social can provide additional insights, especially for cross-platform analysis.

5. Setting and Tracking Goals

- **Define Clear Goals**: Set specific, measurable goals (e.g., increase follower count by 10% in a month).

- **Track Progress**: Regularly check your analytics to monitor progress towards these goals.

6. Understanding User Feedback

- **Sentiment Analysis**: Pay attention to the sentiment in comments and messages to gauge audience perception.

- **Direct Feedback**: Actively seek feedback through polls, surveys, or direct questions.

7. Implementing Insights

- **Strategic Adjustments**: Use the insights from analytics to adjust your content strategy, posting schedule, and engagement tactics.

- **Experimentation**: Don't be afraid to experiment with new types of content or different posting times based on your analytics insights.

Conclusion

Understanding social media analytics is about more than just tracking numbers; it's about gaining insights into your audience's preferences and behaviors, and using that knowledge to make informed decisions about your content and strategy. Regularly reviewing and adapting based on these insights is key to growing your presence and success on social media.

Tools for Better Engagement and Growth on Social Media

In the dynamic world of social media, leveraging the right tools can significantly enhance your engagement and growth. These tools can help in scheduling content, analyzing performance, managing interactions, and more. Here's an overview of various tools that can aid in boosting your social media presence:

1. Content Scheduling and Management Tools

- **Hootsuite**: Manage multiple social media accounts, schedule posts in advance, and track your social media analytics.

- **Buffer**: A user-friendly tool for scheduling posts, analyzing performance, and managing all your social media accounts in one place.

- **Sprout Social**: Offers comprehensive features for scheduling, analytics, and engagement across various platforms.

2. Analytics and Reporting Tools

- **Google Analytics**: Track and analyze website traffic from your social media channels.

- **SocialBakers**: Provides AI-powered analytics to understand audience behavior and preferences.

- **Keyhole**: Specializes in hashtag analytics and tracking for Twitter and Instagram.

3. Graphic Design and Visual Content Tools

- **Canva**: A user-friendly graphic design tool with templates for social media posts, stories, and ads.

- **Adobe Spark**: Offers professional-grade design tools to create eye-catching social media graphics.

- **PicMonkey**: A photo editing and graphic design tool suitable for creating engaging visual content.

4. Video Creation and Editing Tools

- **InShot**: A mobile app for editing videos with music, text, and effects, perfect for Instagram and TikTok.

- **Filmora**: Offers a range of video editing features suitable for creating high-quality social media content.

- **Animoto**: A tool to create professional-quality videos using templates and a simple drag-and-drop interface.

5. Engagement and Community Management Tools

- **Agorapulse**: Provides tools for managing engagement, content scheduling, reporting, and listening across social networks.

- **Crowdfire**: A social media management tool that helps in content discovery, scheduling, and managing interactions.

- **Mention**: Monitor your brand's presence and engage with your audience across social platforms.

6. Influencer Marketing Platforms

- **BuzzSumo**: Find influencers in your niche and analyze what content performs best for any topic or competitor.

- **AspireIQ (formerly Revfluence)**: Connects brands with influencers for marketing campaigns.

- **Upfluence**: Comprehensive influencer marketing platform that integrates with your social media accounts.

7. SEO and Keyword Tools

- **SEMrush**: Provides tools for SEO, content marketing, competitor research, and more.

- **Ahrefs**: Offers tools for SEO audit, keyword research, and analyzing your competitors' social media strategies.

8. Email Marketing Integration

- **Mailchimp**: Integrate your social media campaigns with email marketing efforts for broader reach.

- **Constant Contact**: Offers tools for email marketing which can be linked with social media activities.

Conclusion

Utilizing these tools can streamline your social media strategy, save time, and provide valuable insights into your audience and performance. By incorporating a mix of scheduling, analytics, content creation, and engagement tools, you can significantly enhance your social media engagement and growth. Remember, the key is to choose tools that best fit your specific needs and goals.

Scheduling and Automation Tools for Social Media

Efficient management of social media often requires the use of scheduling and automation tools. These tools not only save time but also help in maintaining a consistent online presence. By automating certain tasks, you can focus more on creating quality content and engaging with your audience. Here's a guide to some of the most effective scheduling and automation tools available:

1. Hootsuite

- **Features**: Schedule posts across multiple social media platforms, monitor mentions, and track your social media analytics.

- **Best For**: Comprehensive social media management and analytics.

2. Buffer

- **Features**: Easy-to-use interface for scheduling posts, analyzing performance, and managing all your social media accounts.

- **Best For**: Businesses and individuals who need straightforward scheduling and analytics.

3. Sprout Social

- **Features**: Offers features for scheduling, analytics, engagement, and listening across various platforms.

- **Best For**: In-depth analytics and detailed reporting.

4. Later

- **Features**: Visual content calendar, scheduling for posts and stories, and performance analytics, particularly strong for Instagram.

- **Best For**: Visual planning and Instagram management.

5. SocialBee

- **Features**: Schedule posts, categorize content for recycling, and integrate with other tools.

- **Best For**: Content categorization and recycling.

6. CoSchedule

- **Features**: Content calendar, social media scheduling, and analytics. Integrates with blogs and marketing projects.

- **Best For**: Bloggers and marketers who need to integrate social media with content marketing.

7. Agorapulse

- **Features**: Social media scheduling, monitoring, and reporting. Includes a social inbox to manage conversations.

- **Best For**: Comprehensive social media management and customer service.

8. Tailwind

- **Features**: Scheduling tool specifically designed for Pinterest and Instagram. Offers features for smart scheduling, analytics, and content discovery.

- **Best For**: Pinterest and Instagram-focused marketing.

9. Zoho Social

- **Features**: Schedule posts, monitor keywords, collaborate with your team, and analyze performance across social networks.

- **Best For**: Team collaboration and businesses looking for CRM integration.

10. MeetEdgar

- **Features**: Automates content recycling, schedules posts, and provides analytics. Unique in its approach to evergreen content.

- **Best For**: Maximizing the lifespan of your best content.

Conclusion

These scheduling and automation tools can significantly enhance your efficiency and effectiveness on social media. By automating routine tasks, you gain more time to focus on strategy and engagement, which are crucial for social media success. Choose a tool that aligns with your specific needs, whether it's comprehensive platform management, content recycling, team collaboration, or platform-specific features.

Legal and Ethical Considerations in Social Media

N avigating the legal and ethical landscape of social media is crucial for maintaining a responsible online presence and avoiding potential pitfalls. Here's an overview of key areas to consider:

Understanding Platform Policies

- **Platform Terms and Conditions**: Familiarize yourself with the terms of service for each platform you use. These documents outline what is and isn't allowed.

- **Content Guidelines**: Be aware of each platform's content guidelines, including restrictions on hate speech, harassment, and explicit material.

- **Privacy Policies**: Understand how each platform handles user data and what privacy controls are available to you.

Navigating Copyright and Intellectual Property

- **Respecting Copyright Laws**: Ensure that you have the right to use any content you post, including images, videos, and music. Unauthorized use can lead to legal issues.

- **Creative Commons Licensing**: Utilize content available under Creative Commons licenses if you do not own content but ensure to adhere to the specified licensing terms.

- **Fair Use Doctrine**: Be aware of the fair use doctrine, which allows limited use of copyrighted material without permission for purposes like commentary, news reporting, or research.

- **Intellectual Property of Your Own Content**: Understand your rights regarding the content you create and how it can be used by others.

Ethical Advertising and Sponsorships

- **Transparency in Sponsorships**: Clearly disclose any sponsorships or paid partnerships in your content. Viewers and followers should be able to distinguish between paid and organic content easily.

- **Honest Endorsements**: Only endorse or promote products

or services you genuinely believe in. Misleading endorsements can erode trust and have legal ramifications.

- **Adhering to Advertising Standards**: Follow the advertising standards and guidelines set forth by regulatory bodies in your region (like the FTC in the USA).

Conclusion

In the world of social media, staying informed about legal and ethical considerations is as crucial as your content strategy. Respecting platform policies, copyright laws, and ethical standards in advertising not only helps in maintaining a positive online presence but also safeguards you from potential legal issues. As social media continues to evolve, keeping abreast of these aspects is necessary for responsible and successful online engagement.

Case Studies and Success Stories

Facebook Success Stories

1. **Humans of New York (HONY)**: Started by Brandon Stanton, HONY began as a photography project and evolved into a Facebook page sharing stories of people in New York City. It has since grown into a global phenomenon, leading to book deals and worldwide recognition.

2. **Chewbacca Mom**: Candace Payne's simple video of herself joyously wearing a Chewbacca mask became one of the most viewed Facebook Live videos at the time, leading to numerous talk show appearances and deals.

Instagram Success Stories

1. **Kayla Itsines**: A personal trainer from Australia, Kayla utilized Instagram to promote her fitness programs. Her Bikini Body Guides (BBG) and Sweat app gained a massive following, turning her into a multi-million-dollar brand.

2. **Doug the Pug**: This account shows how a pet can become a social media sensation. Doug the Pug's Instagram fame led to a book deal, merchandise, and numerous brand partnerships.

TikTok Success Stories

1. **Charli D'Amelio**: Starting as a regular user, Charli became a TikTok sensation for her dance videos. She amassed millions of followers in a short time, leading to brand deals, a Super Bowl commercial, and even a TV show.

2. **Zach King**: Known for his "magic vines," Zach King's creative and illusion-based videos on TikTok have garnered a massive following and led to collaborations with various brands and entertainment opportunities.

Twitter Success Stories

1. **Wendy's**: Known for its witty and sometimes sarcastic Twitter presence, Wendy's leveraged the platform for brand engagement. Their unique tone and engagement with users have set them apart in social media marketing.

2. **Jonny Sun**: An author and illustrator, Jonny Sun gained

popularity with his relatable and humorous tweets. His unique Twitter voice led to a book deal and several writing opportunities in TV and film.

Cross-Platform Success Stories

1. **Tasty by BuzzFeed**: Starting on Facebook, Tasty's simple, quick recipe videos went viral, leading to immense popularity across various social platforms including Instagram and YouTube, and eventually to a line of cookware.

2. **Gary Vaynerchuk**: A serial entrepreneur, Gary leveraged platforms like Twitter, Facebook, and Instagram to build his personal brand. His consistent content strategy across social media led to successful businesses, speaking engagements, and a significant online following.

Each of these cases demonstrates how creativity, consistency, and engagement with the audience can lead to extraordinary success on social media platforms. They highlight the power of social media in building brands, creating opportunities, and reaching a global audience.

Analysis of Successful Monetization Strategies on Social Media

The digital landscape of social media provides numerous avenues for monetization, each requiring its own strategy and approach. By analyzing successful monetization strategies, we can glean insights into what works and why. Here's a breakdown of effective strategies across various platforms:

1. Diversification of Revenue Streams

- **Key Insight**: Relying on a single monetization method can be risky. Successful social media personalities and businesses often diversify their income sources.

- **Examples**: This can include a mix of sponsored content, affiliate marketing, selling products or services, and utilizing platform-specific monetization features like YouTube's Partner Program or TikTok's Creator Fund.

2. Leveraging Personal Brand

- **Key Insight**: A strong, relatable personal brand can attract sponsorships and partnerships.

- **Examples**: Influencers like Huda Kattan or Gary Vaynerchuk have leveraged their personal brand to partner with companies, launch their own product lines, or offer paid consultations.

3. Engaging Content that Adds Value

- **Key Insight**: Content that entertains, informs, or solves problems tends to attract and retain a loyal audience, which is attractive to advertisers.

- **Examples**: Educational platforms like Khan Academy or entertainment-centric channels like Dude Perfect on YouTube.

4. Utilizing Platform-Specific Features

- **Key Insight**: Each social media platform offers unique features that can be optimized for monetization.

- **Examples**: Instagram influencers often use Instagram Shopping to tag products in their posts, while businesses on Facebook make use of Facebook Shops and Marketplace.

5. Community Building and Engagement

- **Key Insight**: Building a community and regularly engaging with followers can lead to higher loyalty and better monetization opportunities.

- **Examples**: Twitch streamers often build a sense of community among their viewers, leading to donations, subscriptions, and merchandise sales.

6. Strategic Use of Analytics

- **Key Insight**: Successful monetization often involves analyzing social media metrics to understand what content works best.

- **Examples**: Creators use insights from Instagram or Facebook Analytics to tailor their content strategy to their audience's preferences, improving engagement and sponsorship opportunities.

7. Adaptability and Trend Utilization

- **Key Insight**: Adapting to new trends and platform changes quickly can give a competitive edge.

- **Examples**: TikTok stars like Charli D'Amelio gained popularity by quickly jumping on trending dances and challenges.

8. Cross-Promotion Across Platforms

- **Key Insight**: Utilizing multiple platforms to cross-promote content can amplify reach and open up additional revenue channels.

- **Examples**: YouTubers often use Instagram or Twitter to drive traffic to their YouTube content, increasing ad revenue.

9. Authenticity in Sponsored Content

- **Key Insight**: Transparency and authenticity in sponsored content can maintain audience trust and lead to more successful brand partnerships.

- **Examples**: Creators who disclose sponsored content clearly and promote products that align with their personal brand tend to have better audience receptivity.

10. Niche Specialization

- **Key Insight**: Focusing on a specific niche can attract a dedicated following, which is often more lucrative for targeted advertising and sponsorships.

- **Examples**: Fitness influencers, gaming content creators, or beauty vloggers often find success in attracting niche-specific sponsorships.

Conclusion

The crux of successful monetization on social media lies in understanding the unique aspects of each platform, building a loyal audience, and maintaining authenticity and engagement. Diversification of income streams, leveraging personal branding, and adapting to changing trends also play a crucial role in monetizing social media effectively.

Common Challenges in Social Media Monetization and Overcoming Obstacles

Monetizing social media can be a rewarding venture, but it comes with its own set of challenges. Recognizing these challenges and finding ways to overcome them is crucial for long-term success and staying motivated. Here's a look at some common obstacles in social media monetization and strategies to address them:

9.1 Common Challenges in Social Media Monetization

1. **Saturation of the Market**: As more people turn to social media for monetization, the competition gets fiercer.

2. **Changing Algorithms**: Social media platforms frequently change their algorithms, affecting content visibility and engagement.

3. **Building and Retaining Audience**: Continuously attracting and keeping your audience's attention in a constantly evolving space.

4. **Content Creation Burnout**: Consistently producing fresh, engaging content can be exhausting.

5. **Maintaining Authenticity**: Balancing sponsored content and genuine posts without alienating your audience.

6. **Platform Dependency**: Relying too heavily on a single platform for revenue can be risky.

7. **Adhering to Legal and Ethical Standards**: Navigating the complexities of legal and ethical considerations in digital marketing.

9.2 Overcoming Obstacles and Staying Motivated

1. **Differentiation**: Stand out by creating unique, high-quality content. Carve out a niche where you can excel.

2. **Adaptability**: Stay informed about platform changes and

adapt your strategies accordingly. Flexibility is key.

3. **Community Engagement**: Focus on building a community around your brand. Engage with your audience consistently to foster loyalty.

4. **Content Planning**: Develop a content calendar and schedule to avoid burnout. It's important to take regular breaks and manage your workload.

5. **Balance in Monetization**: Find a balance between sponsored and organic content. Always prioritize the value for your audience.

6. **Diversify Income Sources**: Expand your monetization channels beyond one platform. Explore merchandise, digital products, Patreon, etc.

7. **Stay Informed**: Keep up-to-date with legal requirements like disclosure guidelines and copyright laws to ensure compliance.

8. **Set Realistic Goals**: Establish achievable goals and track your progress. Celebrate small victories to stay motivated.

9. **Seek Support**: Join communities or networks of social media professionals. Learning from others can provide new insights and inspiration.

10. **Continuous Learning**: Embrace the learning curve. Attend webinars, read relevant articles, and stay curious about new trends and tactics.

Conclusion

Navigating the challenges of social media monetization requires a combination of creativity, strategic planning, and adaptability. By understanding the potential obstacles and implementing effective strategies to overcome them, you can maintain a sustainable and rewarding presence on social media. Remember, staying motivated and resilient in the face of challenges is key to long-term success.

Future Trends in Social Media Monetization

T he landscape of social media is continuously evolving, presenting new trends and opportunities for monetization. Understanding these trends and adapting to changes is crucial for staying relevant and successful. Here's an insight into future trends and strategies to stay ahead of the curve:

Emerging Platforms and Opportunities

1. **Rise of New Platforms**: Platforms like Clubhouse and Discord are gaining traction, offering fresh avenues for monetization through their unique features.

2. **E-Commerce Integration**: Enhanced e-commerce features within social media platforms, like Instagram Shops and

Facebook Marketplace, are transforming social selling.

3. **Augmented Reality (AR) and Virtual Reality (VR)**: As AR and VR technologies develop, expect more immersive advertising and shopping experiences on social media.

4. **AI and Personalization**: AI-driven personalization will offer more targeted advertising opportunities, improving efficiency in reaching the right audience.

5. **Micro-Influencer Focus**: Brands are increasingly collaborating with micro-influencers for their highly engaged audiences.

6. **Video Content Dominance**: Continued dominance of video content, especially short-form videos, as seen with the rise of TikTok and Instagram Reels.

7. **Interactive and Live Content**: Growing popularity of live streaming and interactive content for real-time engagement.

8. **Subscription Models**: Platforms like Twitter and Patreon are exploring subscription models, providing content creators with a direct income stream from their audience.

Staying Ahead of the Curve: Adapting to Changes

1. **Continuous Learning**: Stay updated with industry trends, new platform features, and digital marketing strategies.

2. **Experimentation**: Be open to experimenting with new platforms and content formats to see what resonates best

with your audience.

3. **Audience Feedback**: Regularly seek and listen to audience feedback to understand their evolving preferences.

4. **Network with Peers**: Connect with other social media professionals to share insights and learn from their experiences.

5. **Diversify Your Strategy**: Don't rely on a single platform or monetization method. Diversifying can safeguard against sudden platform changes.

6. **Invest in Technology**: Embrace new technologies like AR, VR, and AI tools that can enhance your content and advertising strategies.

7. **Training and Development**: Invest in training courses or workshops to enhance your skills in areas like video production, SEO, or data analytics.

8. **Monitor Competitors**: Keep an eye on your competitors and industry leaders to learn from their adaptations to market changes.

9. **User Experience Focus**: Prioritize creating a seamless and enjoyable user experience in all your monetization efforts.

Conclusion

The future of social media monetization is marked by rapid technological advancements, shifting user behaviors, and the emergence of new platforms. To capitalize on these changes, it's crucial to stay informed, be adaptable, and continuously engage with your audience. By embracing innovation and maintaining a flexible approach, you can stay ahead in the dynamic world of social media.

Conclusion and Next Steps in Social Media Monetization

As we conclude our exploration of social media monetization, it's important to recap the key strategies that can lead to success. Additionally, I'll provide an action plan to help you get started on your journey.

Recap of Key Strategies

1. **Understanding Each Platform**: Familiarize yourself with the unique features and audiences of each social media platform.

2. **Content Creation and Consistency**: Develop a content strategy that resonates with your audience and maintain a consistent posting schedule.

3. **Engaging with Your Audience**: Build a community by regularly interacting with your followers.

4. **Utilizing Analytics**: Use analytics tools to track performance and understand your audience better.

5. **Diversification of Revenue Streams**: Explore various monetization methods such as sponsored content, affiliate marketing, selling products or services, and ads.

6. **Staying Up-to-Date**: Keep abreast of the latest trends, platform updates, and emerging technologies in social media.

7. **Legal and Ethical Compliance**: Adhere to platform policies and maintain transparency and ethical practices in your monetization efforts.

8. **Continuous Learning and Adaptation**: Be prepared to adapt your strategies in response to changing trends and audience feedback.

Action Plan for Getting Started

1. **Set Clear Goals**: Define what you want to achieve with social media monetization, whether it's building your brand, increasing sales, or earning through content creation.

2. **Choose Your Platforms**: Based on your goals and audience,

select the platforms that best suit your needs.

3. **Create or Optimize Your Profiles**: Ensure your social media profiles are complete, professional, and aligned with your brand.

4. **Develop a Content Strategy**: Plan your content types, themes, and posting schedule.

5. **Start Creating and Posting Content**: Begin posting content, keeping consistency and quality in mind.

6. **Engage with Your Audience**: Actively respond to comments, messages, and engage with other users' content.

7. **Monitor Your Progress**: Regularly check your analytics to see what's working and what isn't.

8. **Explore Monetization Options**: Once you have built a decent following, start exploring different monetization methods available on each platform.

9. **Network and Collaborate**: Connect with other creators or businesses for potential partnerships or collaborations.

10. **Review and Adjust**: Continuously review your strategies and make necessary adjustments based on your performance and audience feedback.

Conclusion

Entering the world of social media monetization is an exciting journey that requires creativity, adaptability, and persistence. By following these strategies and action steps, you can build a strong online presence and start monetizing your social media platforms effectively. Remember, success in social media is a gradual process, and staying committed to your goals while being open to learning and adapting is key.

Appendices

Appendices

A. Useful Resources and Tools

1. Content Creation

- **Canva**: For creating social media graphics.

- **Adobe Spark**: For professional-grade graphic design.

2. Video Editing

- **InShot**: Handy for editing social media videos.

- **Filmora**: Offers advanced video editing features.

3. Social Media Management

- **Hootsuite**: For scheduling posts and tracking analytics.

- **Buffer**: Simplifies post scheduling and performance analysis.

4. Analytics Tools

- **Google Analytics**: For tracking website traffic from social media.

- **SocialBakers**: AI-powered analytics tool for audience insights.

5. SEO and Keyword Research

- **SEMrush**: Comprehensive SEO toolkit.

- **Ahrefs**: For SEO analysis and keyword research.

6. Email Marketing

- **Mailchimp**: Integrates email campaigns with social media.

- **Constant Contact**: Email marketing service with social media features.

7. Influencer Marketing Platforms

- **AspireIQ**: Connects brands with influencers.

- **BuzzSumo**: For finding influencers and analyzing content.

8. Graphic Design and Photo Editing

- **PicMonkey**: Online photo editing and design service.

- **GIMP**: Free alternative for advanced photo editing.

9. Learning Resources

- **Social Media Examiner**: Offers latest social media marketing tips.

- **HubSpot Academy**: Provides free online training courses.

B. Glossary of Terms

1. **Engagement Rate**: A metric that measures the level of engagement (likes, comments, shares) that content receives relative to the audience size.

2. **Reach**: The total number of unique users who see your content.

3. **Impressions**: The number of times your content is displayed, regardless of whether it was clicked.

4. **Click-Through Rate (CTR)**: The ratio of users who click on a specific link to the number of total users who view a page, email, or advertisement.

5. **Conversion Rate**: The percentage of visitors who take the desired action.

6. **Hashtag**: A word or phrase preceded by a hash sign (#), used on social media sites to identify messages on a specific topic.

7. **Algorithm**: A set of rules that social media platforms use to determine which content to display to users.

8. **Content Calendar**: A schedule of when and where to pub-

lish upcoming content.

9. **Influencer**: A social media user who can influence potential buyers of a product or service.

10. **Affiliate Marketing**: A marketing arrangement by which an online retailer pays commission to an external website for traffic or sales generated from its referrals.

11. **Sponsored Content**: Content created specifically to promote a product or service, for which the creator is typically paid by the brand.

References and Further Reading

To deepen your understanding of social media monetization and stay updated with the latest trends and strategies, here are some recommended resources and books. These references are valuable for both beginners and experienced social media users:

Books

1. **"Jab, Jab, Jab, Right Hook" by Gary Vaynerchuk**: Offers insights into creating compelling content tailored for each social media platform.

2. **"Crushing It!: How Great Entrepreneurs Build Their Business and Influence-and How You Can, Too" by Gary Vaynerchuk**: Provides strategies for personal branding and leveraging social media for business growth.

3. **"Social Media Marketing Workbook: How to Use So-

cial Media for Business" by Jason McDonald Ph.D.: A workbook offering practical steps to develop a social media marketing strategy.

4. **"Influence: Building a Platform that Elevates Jesus (Not Me)" by Kate Motaung and Shannon Popkin**: Focuses on using social media to build a positive and influential platform.

5. **"The Art of Social Media: Power Tips for Power Users" by Guy Kawasaki and Peg Fitzpatrick**: A guide to building a social media brand from two leading industry experts.

Online Resources and Websites

1. **Social Media Examiner**: Provides current news, research, and analysis on social media.

   - Website: socialmediaexaminer.com

2. **HubSpot Blog**: Offers extensive resources on digital marketing, including social media strategies.

   - Website: blog.hubspot.com

3. **Moz Blog**: Excellent resource for learning about SEO and its importance in social media marketing.

   - Website: moz.com/blog

4. **Content Marketing Institute**: Provides insights and tips on content marketing which is integral to social media.

- Website: contentmarketinginstitute.com

5. **Hootsuite Blog**: Offers practical tips and strategies for social media marketing and management.

- Website: blog.hootsuite.com

Podcasts

1. **The GaryVee Audio Experience**: Gary Vaynerchuk shares insights on marketing, social media, and entrepreneurship.

2. **Social Media Marketing Podcast**: Hosted by Michael Stelzner, this podcast offers interviews with social media professionals offering actionable advice.

3. **Online Marketing Made Easy with Amy Porterfield**: Provides tips on digital marketing strategies, including social media.

YouTube Channels

1. **Video Influencers**: Offers tips and strategies for growing your influence with online video and social media.

2. **Brian Dean**: Known for his expertise in SEO, Brian Dean's channel is a great resource for understanding how SEO impacts social media.